MESSENGER

Christy Ducker

with photographs by Kate Sweeney

Published 2017 by
smith|doorstop books
The Poetry Business
Bank Street Arts
32-40 Bank Street
Sheffield S1 2DS

ISBN 978-1-910367-96-4
Designed & typeset by Utter
Cover image by Kate Sweeney
Printed by Biddles Books

smith|doorstop books are a member of Inpress:
www.inpressbooks.co.uk.
Distributed by Central Books Ltd.,
99 Wallis Road, London E9 5LN

The Poetry Business gratefully acknowledges the support
of Arts Council England.

Contents

CII
TC

Acknowledgements

Many thanks to Paul Kaye and Philip Kerrigan, for opening up the residency at York's Centre for Immunology and Infection. A special thank you to Dimitris Lagos, for his generosity, curiosity and imagination whilst overseeing my time at CII – these poems would not have been possible without that extensive dialogue. Thanks also to Michael Plevin, Antal Rot, Marjan van der Woude, and all their lab staff. The last two lines of 'Translation' are Antal Rot's, and are taken from 'Chemokines in Innate and Adaptive Host Defense: Basic Chemokinese Grammar for Immune Cells' (2004) by Ulrich von Andrian & Antal Rot, *Annual Review of Immunology*, 22.891-928. As ever, thanks to all members of the Women's Poetry Workshop at Newcastle University.

for A.P.H.

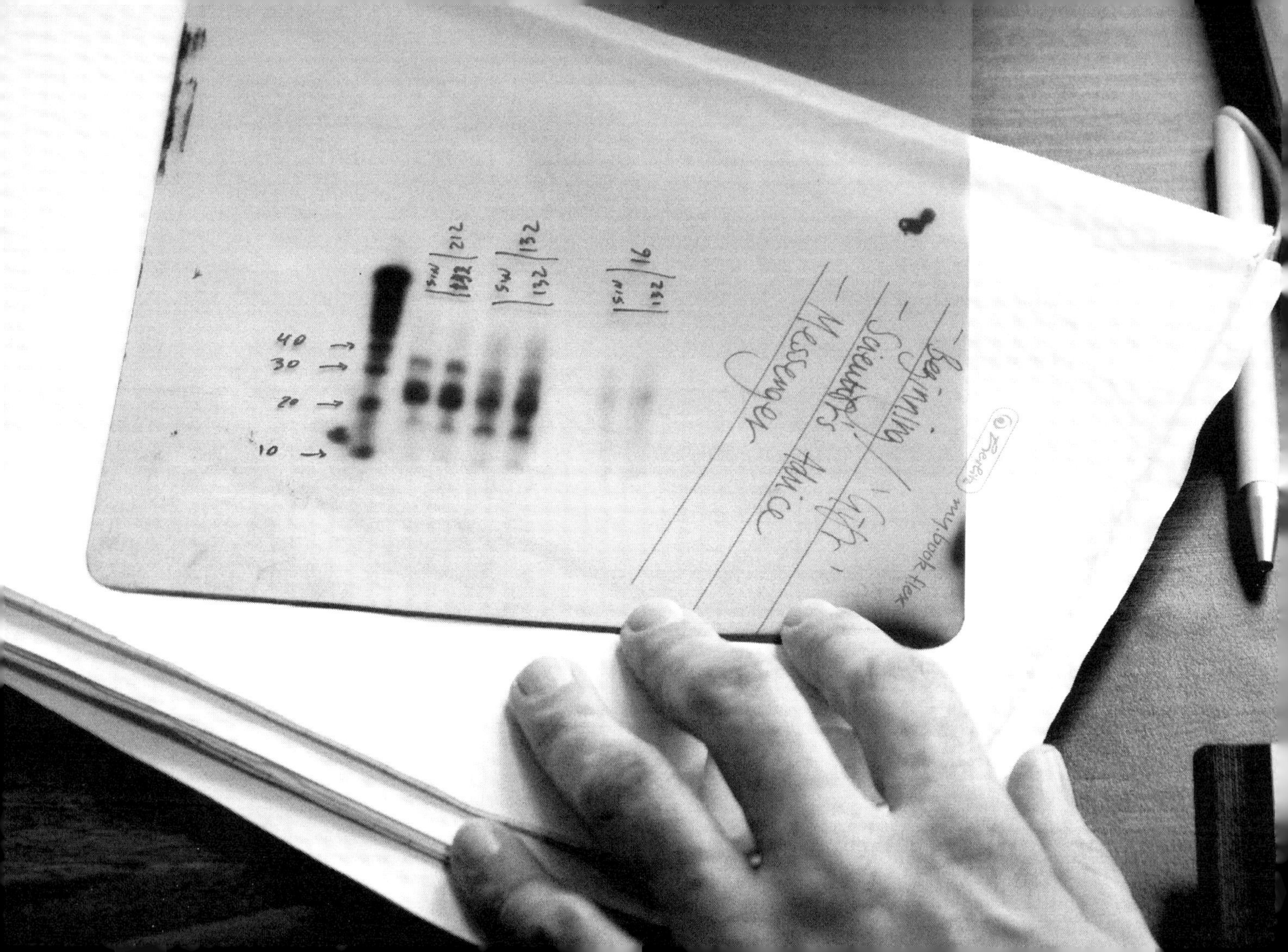
40
30
20
10

Foreword

How wounds heal, how to read the human body, how to invent vaccines, and how to individualize medicine: these are all part of the work that goes on at York's Centre for Immunology and Infection. In 2016, Christy Ducker was poet in residence with us, working alongside medical research scientists to explore and experiment. Her aim was to write about how we wound and how we heal, as people and as communities. The poems in *Messenger* grew from dialogue, and they continue to talk: about what your body is saying, how your genes send messages, and how we might communicate painful experience or difficult times.

Scientists and poets are restless creatures who refuse to accept the inevitable. This comes across in Christy's poems where she gets to grips with the provisionality of healing, its uncertainties and ambivalence. Often, a scientist will say 'we don't know yet', and for a poet this can open up alternative ways of thinking about recovery: sometimes we just have to make friends with our wounds, and understand them from different angles. Christy's poems of loss and hope reflect this, as they range from the microscopic to the global in scope.

Working with Christy, and visual artist Kate Sweeney, I found that science and the arts can help to make each other more social and accessible. It's been a surprise, to see how my everyday experiments can provide the tools a writer needs to make sense of pain. Christy, Kate and I are most grateful to Paul Kaye and Philip Kerrigan for making the residency a possibility, and to the Wellcome Trust for making it a reality.

Dimitris Lagos
Senior Lecturer in Immunology
Medical Research Council New Investigator

DNA

What will you make of this *book*
of life, its three billion letters,
that only you are permitted
to open up and read?

Will you search it for answers,
perhaps turn to the end first?
Or simply become immersed,
let the book float its questions.

I pore over my own copy,
prospecting for tiny signs –
what I'm made of, what might
soothe a particular wound.

In my version, the book rains
instructions I catch on my tongue.
I drink some, and absorb some
idea of a life filling with life.

I'll make of this book myself,
by which I mean a reading
that reimagines feeling pain
how water imagines stone.

A Scientist's Advice on Healing

Try to accept this fat red hurt
as your starting point, in the way

a pen must be put to paper
in one particular spot, then move –

change the subject, before it's too late.
Sketch out what health you still have,

the signal-cascades, and the gangs
of cells that circumnavigate you,

then draw yourself back together
again, in a language of your own.

Your body's talk is loose as lymph –
it'll have you open out as a tree,

or sneak up on pain as assassin,
sidekick, or wolf. Encourage this

when healing won't play straight.
Embrace the lack of heroics –

Messenger

The last message you ever sent still lives
in my old mobile phone – I charge it up,
those odd, inflammatory days when I snap
back to thinking a twist of you might revive,
as if you'd never gone, as if I'd not
become some over-tangled molecule
of grief. The message itself says little,
just blinks in proportion, suggests I *cut
the crap*, *chill out*. Better for now to shush
and switch the phone off, to let you be there
but not there, tucked in my pocket. No rush –
I'm winter's idea of spring, on slow-thaw,
a grizzly bear lumbering through long sleep
while her cells chit-chatter, die off, regroup.

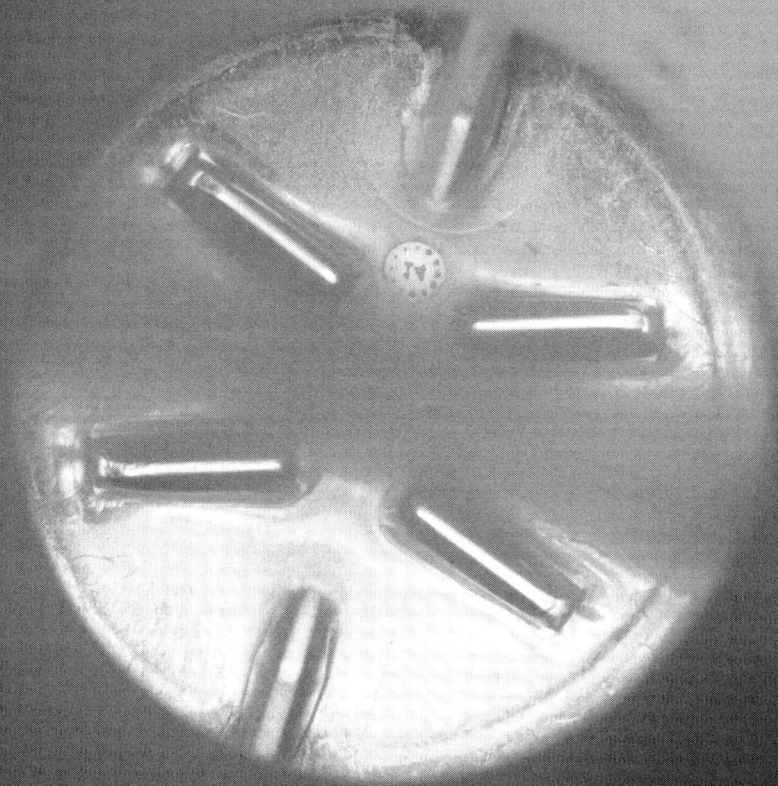

A Baffle

Everything in the lab is moving
towards a clarification
of murk and slosh and life shifting

by way of heat and the shaken
flasks which sweat, tilt and fling cells up
against a baffle, until they spring

their insides (such miniature maps!)
and every hydrophilic grain
sings in its tube of how to adapt,

move on, *get over it. Keep going* –
one way to meet my own baffle,
(that Pennine hill on the skyline

the place where he died, its awful
fact a historic landmark
I knock against) resolve as crystal

refracting the memory. Skylarks
were there that day too, and they sang,
and their nests were still warm after dark.

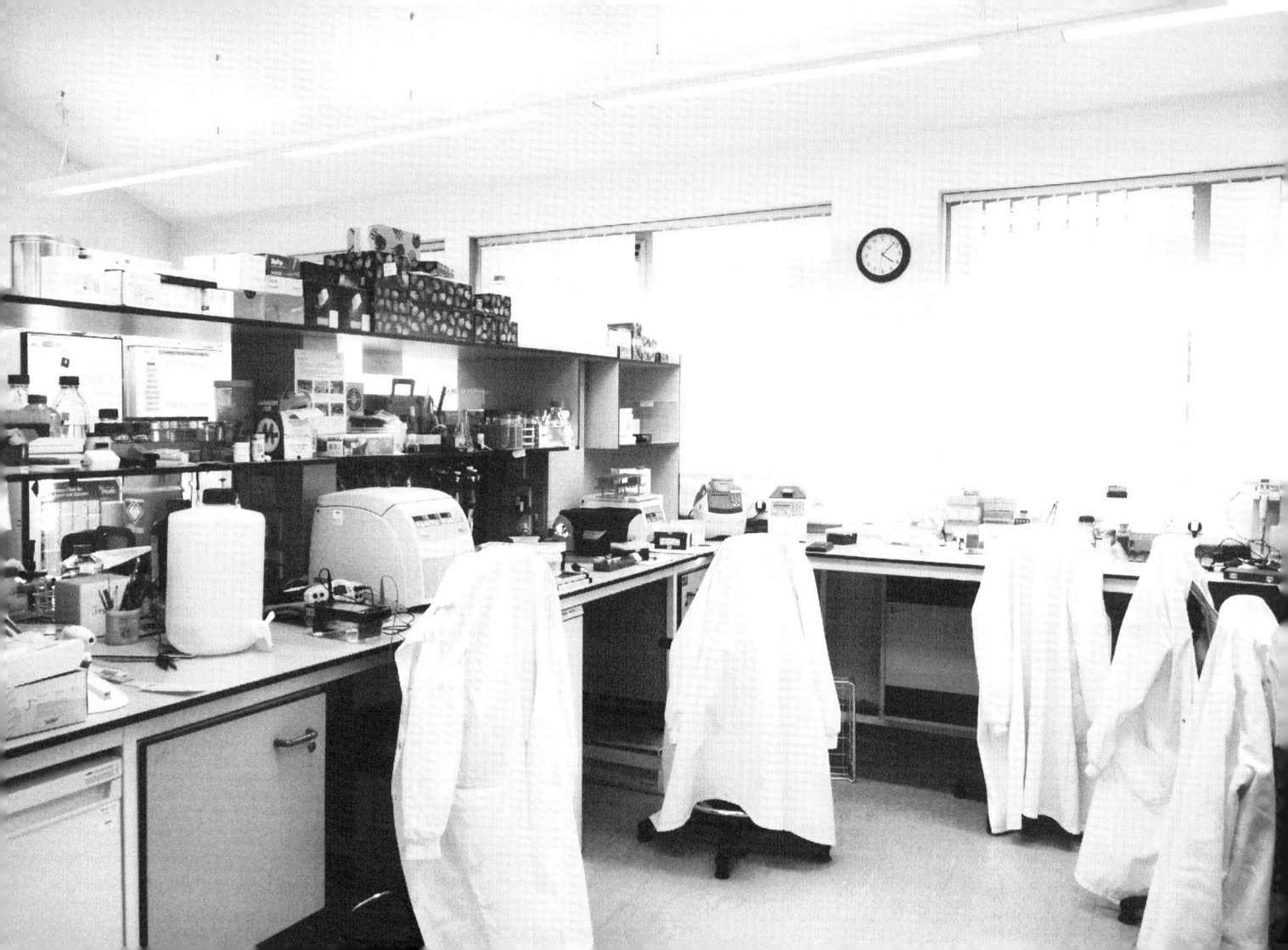

Meanwhile,

imagine you're given a dollar **for every new case of dengue, buruli or yaws**
see it multiply by one and a half billion **amassing in places**
you hadn't thought possible **beyond the headline news**,
would you find it distracting? Imagine **half the children in Kabul**
feeling such ease instead of **never being held again**,
day or night, feeling anxiety grow to **become a disease**
a thing you've been locked into, **more intimate than skin**
or imagine your dollars become a problem **more pertinent than a scar**
marking you out as different, wrong (**maniacal, even**)
maybe you'd rather be given a chance **for every new case of *kala-azar*,**
to belong, and help with healing **a fifth of the world**,
rewrite the tabloids' *FLESH EATING BUGS!* **for the tropically ill**
imagine offering your voice to others **kept on mute –**
or maybe you'd offer money? Or? **Hope and a warning**.

Vaccine

My mother kept me from fairy tales,
not wanting those women in boxes
with all their waiting to stall me,
but when I grew up and found myself
boxed-in, I couldn't see the walls
for years, not having rehearsed horror

in miniature, how a storyteller
or scientist might. Today, in the lab
I learn how to make a horror small,
that we boil it and pin it inside
our own blood, to teach ourselves
the lesson: naivety kills

but memory inoculates, measured out
at the right dose. For lupus, try
absorbing a microgram of its snarl
so you might bite back. For Cinderella
disease, take only its slippers,
appear to swoon but prepare to kick.

The science of self-protection asks
we rewrite the story of what appals:
be glad the hairs on the back of your neck
stir when a wolf comes near you.
For grief, devour a sugar skull
and dance on the Day of the Dead.

Translation

He said there's no point crying,
that life goes on and wounds change.
He said this the way a person will
when they can speak five languages
but rarely go back to their first.
Imagine those refugees on the run
from war, he said. A wound's like that –
it wants to disperse and it won't stop
talking, he said. Your body's fluent
in *chemokinese* – it can haggle its way
to a different state, but it never forgets,
he said. And my body sat there thinking
in chemokinese, trying to parse itself better.
It's all in flux, he said, though the beauty is
your healing is written on sugar.
You're the crib sheet of your own future.

The Enemy

It wasn't that we had grown complacent,
in fact we'd had quite a difficult time,
but the wound was so large and demanding
we had to tend to that. It was only
later we noticed the change of pressure,
that something had come in and squatted us.
It stopped our mouths with what appeared to be
a thin film. We couldn't puncture the stuff.
The usual strategies wouldn't work.
We heard someone on the radio change
the word 'rules' to the word 'witchcraft'.
We tried to learn quickly about the law.

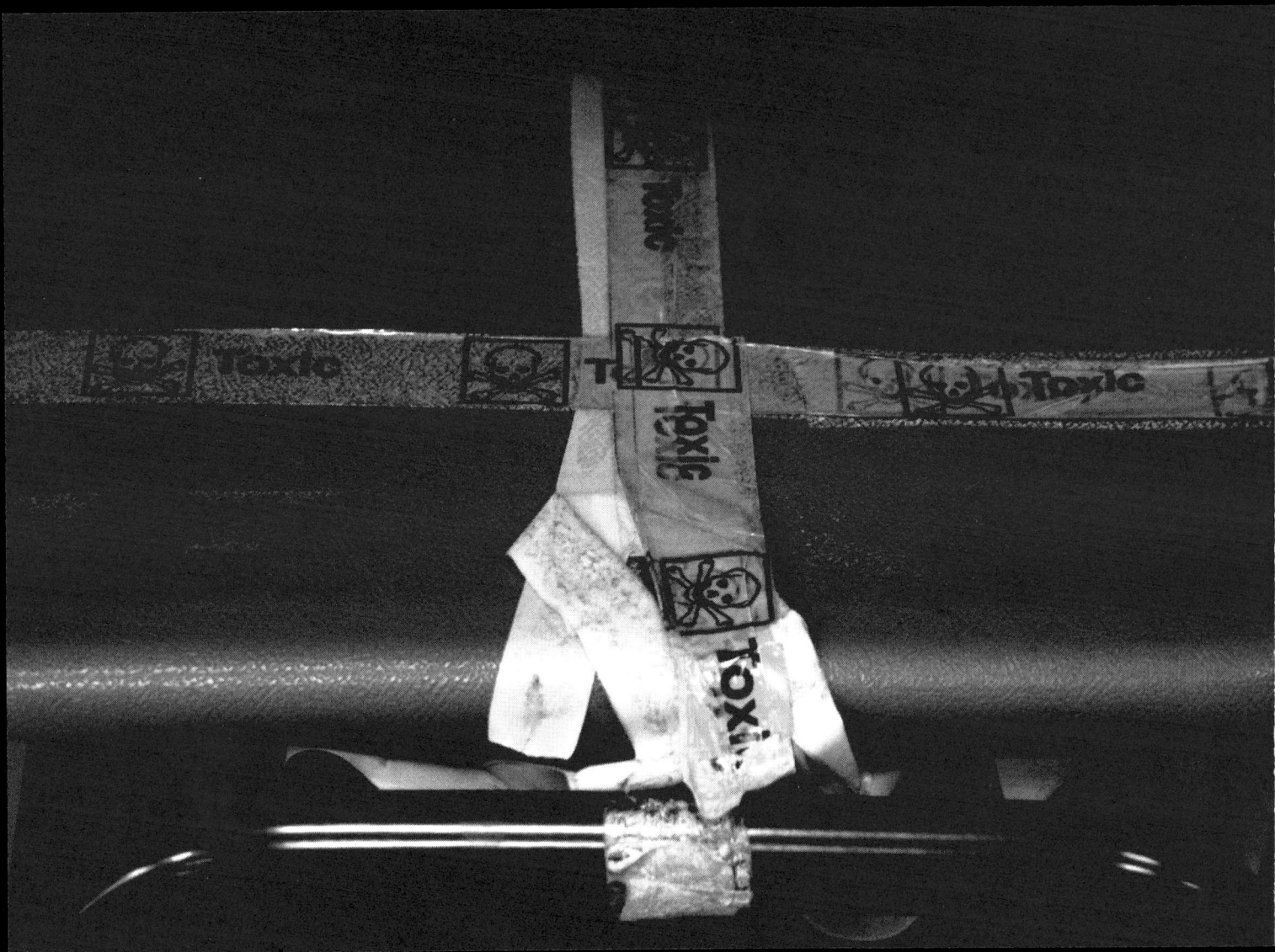

DARC

You've Viking blood, the hairdresser says
as she scrubs at my hairline stained
with dye. *Big bones, blue eyes – always
a sign you'll soak it up more –*

I blink at this news of my thirsty genes,
worry I'm missing something and need
to pillage for colour and heat.
Perhaps this is why I ask a lot –

I ask about the girl from Lodz
who used to work here – *it got too much
for her,* I hear, that *folk can't just rock up
like that – we need to be more*

scientific she says. I think
of what science taught me last week,
about a molecule called DARC.
In this flammable room, I daren't

say how DARC expresses itself
differently by race, that Black health
needs its own answers. Given this,
would she spray it around like anecdote

or be scientific, hold difference
in level hands? Keep evidence
away from hot air and impulse,
rinse the world of all its cancers?

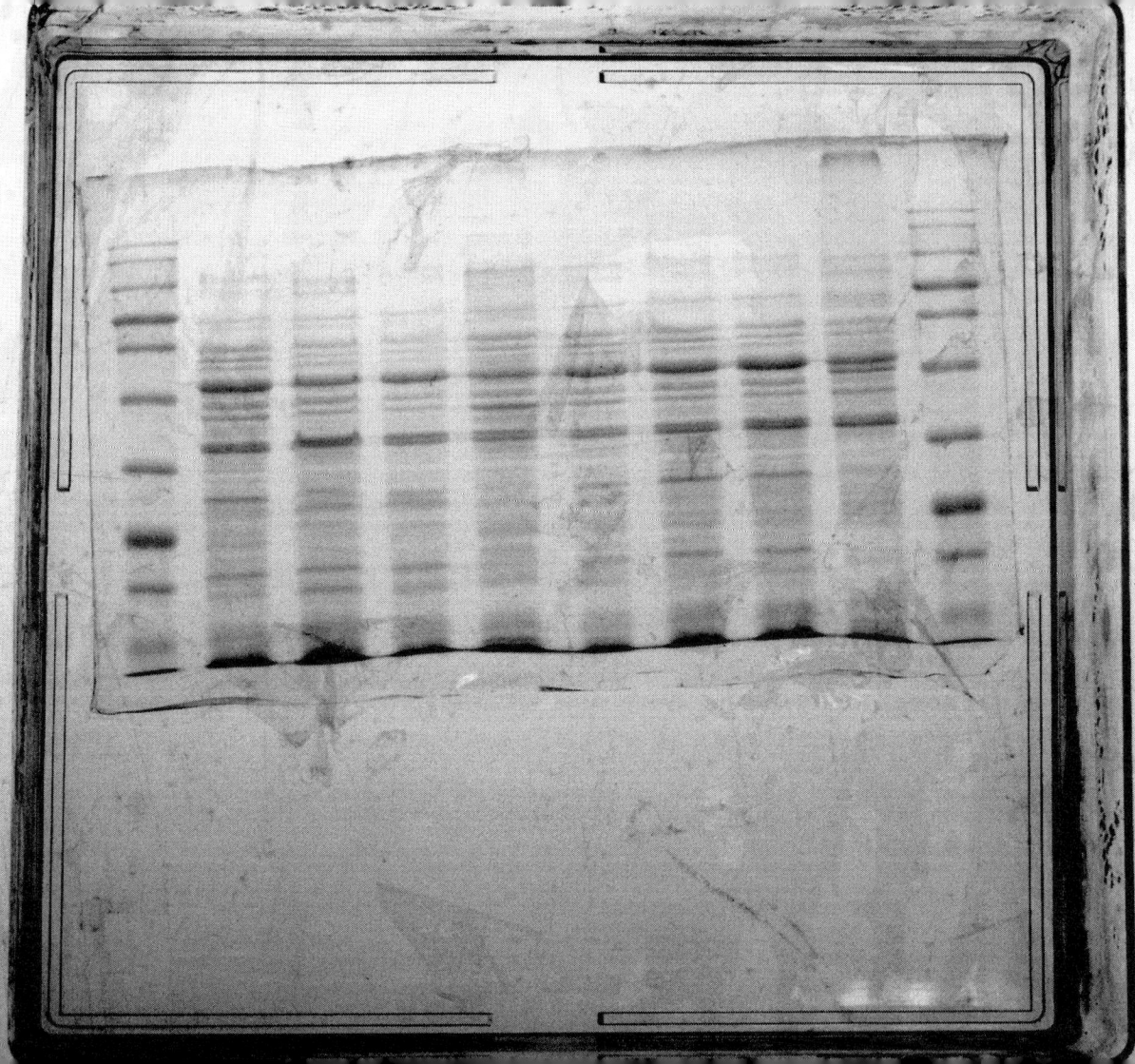

Resolution

Sometimes, it helps to come back to you
in detail, right down to the atoms
that made you, because they were only
ever on loan from the world – true,
if I zoom out a bit, things crazy
to molecules, cells, and how you made
a life for yourself through your hunger
for chatter, people, anywhere noisy,
but sometimes, when you rush back at me,
it helps if I think you really were
just trillions of small parts teetering,
a madcap egg-and-spoon – how lucky
I was, to meet you before you fell
in pieces, to kiss what couldn't hold.

Notes

DNA

DNA (deoxyribonucleic acid) is a long molecule that contains our unique genetic code. Scientists often describe DNA as a 'book' that contains the instructions for making all the proteins in our bodies. Everyone will 'read' that information in their own way, but we'll generally skip about half of the chapters.

A Scientist's Advice on Healing

Healing is not a given, although our immune system will do its best to fight off germs. If we're fairly well, immune cells which help us are the 'assassin' killer T Cells, the helper T Cells, dendritic cells which resemble trees, and macrophage cells which 'wolf' germs whole.

Messenger

Messenger RNA (mRNA) is a molecule which carries information from your DNA to the parts of your cells which make proteins and keep your body ticking over. Sometimes, especially in response to wounds and inflammation, the message from mRNA will be one of calm, a molecular 'Sssshh!' to the body's panic.

A Baffle

When producing proteins in lab conditions, scientists use a baffled flask. The 'baffle' is a raised ridge at the bottom of the flask which speeds up chemical reactions. Murky E. coli solution is sloshed against the baffle, until its molecules begin to break down and the solution clarifies.

Meanwhile,

Around a fifth of the world's population suffer from some form of tropical illness. Many of these illnesses are overlooked by the West, and research into solving them is often underfunded. Scientists at York are trialling a vaccine in the hope of preventing leishmaniasis, a parasitic disease transmitted by sandflies. Leishmaniasis can cause ulceration, and lead to social ostracism. There are approx. 12 million sufferers world-wide at present.

Translation

Chemokinese is a 'language' some molecules use to communicate cell-to-cell and promote healing (amongst many other functions). These communications follow patterns and rules that are reminiscent of grammar. The last two lines of this poem come from a scientific paper by Antal Rot and Ulrich H. von Andrian.

DARC

DARC stands for 'Duffy Antigen Receptor for Chemokines'. It is a molecule located to the outside of some people's red blood cells. If present, it receives communications in chemokinese and passes them on. Depending on our racial heritage, DARC may not be present at all. If it is absent, we're prone to more aggressive forms of some cancers, and more intense experiences of pain. This has significant medical and socio-political implications.

ABOUT THE AUTHOR

Christy Ducker is a poet and tutor. Her first full-length collection, *Skipper*, was published in 2015, and includes work commended by the Forward Prize judges. Her pamphlet, *Armour* (2011), was a PBS Pamphlet Choice. Her commissions include residencies for Port of Tyne, English Heritage, and York University's Centre for Immunology and Infection. She is also the director of *North East Heroes*, an Arts Council England project. Christy is currently REA Fellow at Newcastle University's Institute for Creative Arts Practice.

ABOUT THE ARTIST

Kate Sweeney is a visual artist and videomaker using animation and drawing in her work. She has a collage-like approach, and often works collaboratively with poets, writers and musicians. Kate has exhibited at Sydney International Film Festival, Zebra Film Festival in Berlin, Manchester Animation Festival, and the International Poetry Festival in London. She is currently undertaking a practice-led PhD at Newcastle University. Kate teaches and facilitates art, film and animation in a variety of academic and education contexts.